D0114834

Postcards From Life's Little Instruction Book

by H. Jackson Brown, Jr.

Rutledge Hill Press
Nashville, Tennessee

Published in Nashville, Tennessee by Rutledge Hill Press, Inc.
211 Seventh Avenue North, Nashville, Tennessee 37219.
Distributed in Canada by H.B. Fenn and Company Ltd.,
Mississauga, Ontario.

Printed in Mexico
2 3 4 5 6 7 8 9 — 95 94 93

SEVERAL YEARS AGO I JOTTED DOWN SOME fatherly advice and words of counsel for my son, Adam, as he left home to begin his freshman year at college. Those suggestions were published as *Life's Little Instruction Book*, and to my great surprise and delight it became a number one bestseller.

I still write to Adam on a regular basis and I recently thought how nice it would be to have a series of postcards designed around some of the quotes from the book—a special collection that would offer him continuing encouragement and inspiration.

I asked Jan and Laurie Ellis, two friends of mine and very talented art directors, to design the graphics for 30 of my favorite entries. I think they have done a magnificent job.

I love sending these cards to Adam, other family members, and dear friends. They tell me they save them and put them on bulletin boards, over their desks, and on the most revered place of all, the refrigerator door.

When glancing through this collection, I bet you can think of several people who would love to receive an encouraging note from you. Sending them a postcard is a simple thing to do, but it has the power to make their day simply wonderful.

Don't postpone

JOY.

From *Life's Little Instruction Book*
by H. Jackson Brown, Jr.
Rutledge Hill Press, Nashville, Tennessee

think **big** *Thoughts*

but relish small pleasures.

From *Life's Little Instruction Book*
by H. Jackson Brown, Jr.
Rutledge Hill Press, Nashville, Tennessee

Evaluate yourself by your own standards

not someone else's.

From *Life's Little Instruction Book*
by H. Jackson Brown, Jr.
Rutledge Hill Press, Nashville, Tennessee

Commit Yourself To CONSTANT IMPROVEMENT.

From *Life's Little Instruction Book*
by H. Jackson Brown, Jr.
Rutledge Hill Press, Nashville, Tennessee

Judge your success

by the degree that you're enjoying peace, health, and love.

From *Life's Little Instruction Book*
by H. Jackson Brown, Jr.
Rutledge Hill Press, Nashville, Tennessee

ny time I think of you

my heart smiles w

Never waste an opportunity to tell someone you love them.

u are in my thoughts

I can't wait until

From *Life's Little Instruction Book*
by H. Jackson Brown, Jr.
Rutledge Hill Press, Nashville, Tennessee

NEVER

*take action
when you're*

ANGRY.

From *Life's Little Instruction Book*
by H. Jackson Brown, Jr.
Rutledge Hill Press, Nashville, Tennessee

GET YOUR PRIORITIES STRAIGHT.

No one ever said on his death bed, "Gee, if I'd only spent more time at the office."

From *Life's Little Instruction Book*
by H. Jackson Brown, Jr.
Rutledge Hill Press, Nashville, Tennessee

Go the distance.

*When you accept a task,
finish it.*

From *Life's Little Instruction Book*
by H. Jackson Brown, Jr.
Rutledge Hill Press, Nashville, Tennessee

Never underestimate the power of a

KIND WORD

or deed.

From *Life's Little Instruction Book*
by H. Jackson Brown, Jr.
Rutledge Hill Press, Nashville, Tennessee

Learn to
Listen.
Opportunity sometimes knocks very softly.

From *Life's Little Instruction Book*
by H. Jackson Brown, Jr.
Rutledge Hill Press, Nashville, Tennessee

MAKE IT A HABIT TO
DO NICE
THINGS
FOR PEOPLE WHO'LL NEVER
FIND OUT.

From *Life's Little Instruction Book*
by H. Jackson Brown, Jr.
Rutledge Hill Press, Nashville, Tennessee

Don't Flaunt Your Success.

[BUT DON'T APOLOGIZE FOR IT EITHER.]

From *Life's Little Instruction Book*
by H. Jackson Brown, Jr.

Rutledge Hill Press, Nashville, Tennessee

NEVER CUT WHAT CAN BE UNTIED.

From *Life's Little Instruction Book*
by H. Jackson Brown, Jr.
Rutledge Hill Press, Nashville, Tennessee

Every
So Often
Push Your
Luck.

From *Life's Little Instruction Book*
by H. Jackson Brown, Jr.
Rutledge Hill Press, Nashville, Tennessee

Become the most

positive

AND

enthusiastic

person you know.

From *Life's Little Instruction Book*
by H. Jackson Brown, Jr.
Rutledge Hill Press, Nashville, Tennessee

TAKE CARE OF YOUR REPUTATION

IT'S YOUR MOST VALUABLE ASSET.

From *Life's Little Instruction Book*
by H. Jackson Brown, Jr.
Rutledge Hill Press, Nashville, Tennessee

DO BATTLE

AGAINST PREJUDICE

AND DISCRIMINATION

WHEREVER YOU

FIND IT.

From *Life's Little Instruction Book*
by H. Jackson Brown, Jr.

Rutledge Hill Press, Nashville, Tennessee

BE BRAVE

EVEN IF YOU'RE NOT, PRETEND TO BE. NO ONE CAN TELL THE DIFFERENCE.

From *Life's Little Instruction Book*
by H. Jackson Brown, Jr.
Rutledge Hill Press, Nashville, Tennessee

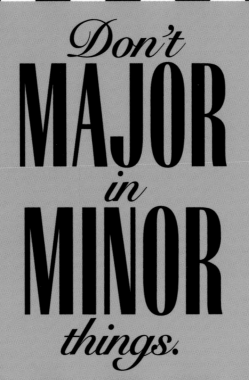

From *Life's Little Instruction Book*
by H. Jackson Brown, Jr.
Rutledge Hill Press, Nashville, Tennessee

PRAY

NOT FOR THINGS BUT FOR WISDOM AND COURAGE.

From *Life's Little Instruction Book*
by H. Jackson Brown, Jr.
Rutledge Hill Press, Nashville, Tennessee

NEVER GIVE UP
ON ANYBODY.
MIRACLES
HAPPEN EVERY DAY.

From *Life's Little Instruction Book*
by H. Jackson Brown, Jr.
Rutledge Hill Press, Nashville, Tennessee

BE DECISIVE

EVEN IF IT MEANS YOU'LL SOMETIMES BE WRONG.

From *Life's Little Instruction Book*
by H. Jackson Brown, Jr.
Rutledge Hill Press, Nashville, Tennessee

*Leave
everything a little*
better
than you found it.

From *Life's Little Instruction Book*
by H. Jackson Brown, Jr.
Rutledge Hill Press, Nashville, Tennessee

NEVER
COMPROMISE
YOUR
INTEGRITY.

From *Life's Little Instruction Book*
by H. Jackson Brown, Jr.
Rutledge Hill Press, Nashville, Tennessee

*Leave
everything a little*
better
than you found it.

From *Life's Little Instruction Book*
by H. Jackson Brown, Jr.
Rutledge Hill Press, Nashville, Tennessee

When someone **Hugs** you, let them be the first to let go.

From *Life's Little Instruction Book*
by H. Jackson Brown, Jr.
Rutledge Hill Press, Nashville, Tennessee

Never deprive someone of

HOPE.

It might be all they have.

From *Life's Little Instruction Book*
by H. Jackson Brown, Jr.
Rutledge Hill Press, Nashville, Tennessee

COMPLIMENT
THREE PEOPLE
EVERY DAY.

From *Life's Little Instruction Book*
by H. Jackson Brown, Jr.
Rutledge Hill Press, Nashville, Tennessee

BE BOLD

AND COURAGEOUS.

❦ WHEN YOU LOOK BACK ON YOUR LIFE, YOU'LL REGRET THE THINGS YOU DIDN'T DO MORE THAN THE ONES YOU DID. ❦❦

From *Life's Little Instruction Book*
by H. Jackson Brown, Jr.
Rutledge Hill Press, Nashville, Tennessee

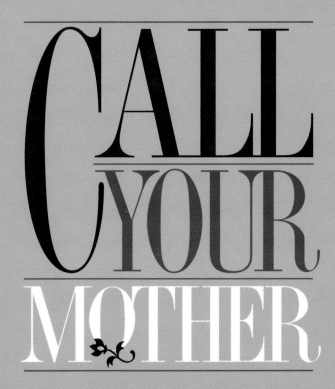

From *Life's Little Instruction Book*
by H. Jackson Brown, Jr.
Rutledge Hill Press, Nashville, Tennessee